FRONTIERSMEN OF AMERICA

Daniel Boone

IN THE WILDERNESS

MATTHEW G. GRANT

Illustrated by Harold Henriksen

GALLERY OF GREAT AMERICANS SERIES

Daniel Boone

IN THE WILDERNESS

Library of Congress Number: 73-10063   ISBN: O-87191-253-8

Published by Creative Education, Mankato, Minnesota 56001
Distributed by Childrens Press, 1224 West Van Buren Street, Chicago, Illinois 60607

Library of Congress Cataloging in Publication Data
Grant, Matthew G.
   Daniel Boone in the wilderness.
                         (Gallery of great Americans)
   SUMMARY: A brief biography of the famed frontiersman who led settlers into Kentucky, was elected to the Kentucky assembly, and lost his own land there in disastrous legal battles.
   1. Boone, Daniel, 1734-1820—Juvenile literature. [1. Boone, Daniel, 1734-1829. 2. Frontier and pioneer life] I. Title. F454.G72 1974 976.9'02'0924 [B] [92] 73-10070
ISBN 0-87191-256-2

CONTENTS

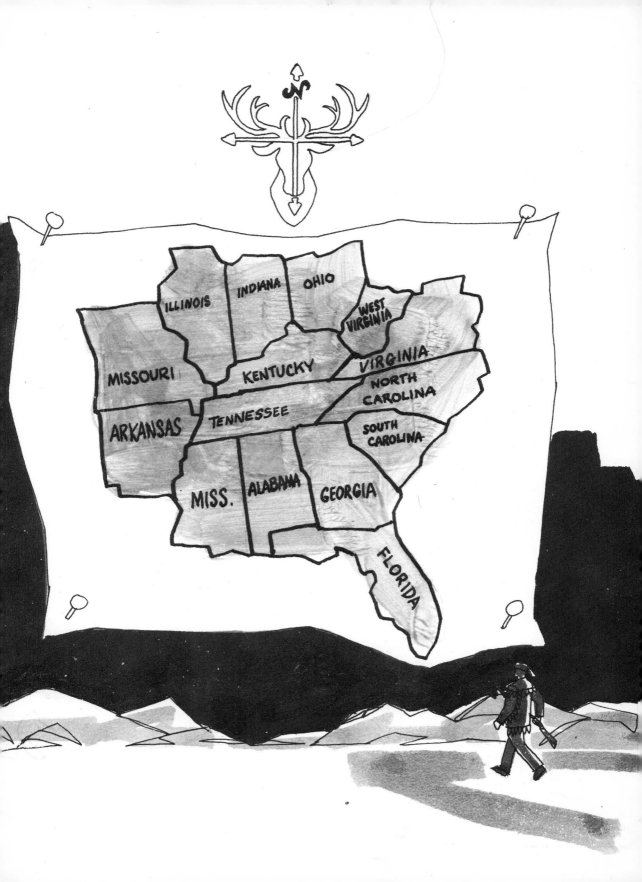

THE YOUNG WOODSMAN

The Boone family were settlers in Pennsylvania. The land was rich and the Indians were friendly. This was because the red men had been paid well for the land taken by the white pioneers.

Squire Boone and his wife Sarah lived in a log cabin in Berks County. They kept cattle, and they also had a small weaving and blacksmith shop.

Their sixth son, Daniel, was born in 1734. The boy roamed the wilderness from the time he could first walk. He made friends with the Delaware Indians. From them, he learned how to stalk wild game and how to survive in the deep forest.

Young Daniel Boone got his first musket when he was thirteen. He quickly became a crack shot. But when it was time to study reading and writing, he would disappear!

"Never mind," said Squire Boone. "Let the girls do the spelling and Dan will do the shooting."

"I can learn more from the Indians than from going to school," Daniel Boone said.

The Boone family moved to North Carolina when Daniel was 16. The new land was fertile. But raiding Indians came from the West and attacked the settlers. The French were stirring up a war because they wanted land that the British claimed.

Young Daniel Boone drove a supply wagon during the French and Indian War that began in 1754. He probably fought with General John Forbes.

In 1756, Daniel married Rebecca Bryan. They bought farm land. But Daniel did not really want to be a farmer. His heart longed for the wilderness. He wandered through the mountains, hunting and exploring. In many places he carved messages on trees that were still there 100 years later. One of them read:

D. BOON CILLED A BAR ON TREE IN THE YEAR 1760

D BOON
CILLED
A
BAR ON
TREE IN
THE YEAR
1760

THE WILDERNESS ROAD

In 1769, Daniel Boone was unhappy. North Carolina was getting too tame. Taxes were high. An old friend named John Finley said: "Let's go to Kentucky! A man can get rich there!"

They went over the Cumberland Mountains and found a marvelous new land. Boone came back and told people about it. He tried to get a wealthy man named Richard Henderson to buy Kentucky from the Indians and open it to settlers.

But Henderson was too busy with other matters. So Boone decided to lead pioneers to the new land himself. He set out with 40 people in 1773.

Indians attacked them. Several were killed, including Boone's small son, James. Most of the people went back to North Carolina.

But Daniel Boone did
not give up his plan. Finally,
in 1775, Richard Henderson
bought Kentucky from the Cherokee Indians
for 10,000 pounds. Daniel Boone and a crew
of men began to build a Wilderness Road for
settlers to follow.

DARK AND BLOODY GROUND

The wagons of settlers rumbled down the Wilderness Road. At its end, on the Kentucky River, was a new little town named Boonesborough. Boone's own family were among the first to live there.

Far away to the east, American colonists were rebelling against the British government. But the people in Kentucky had other things to worry about.

In the summer of 1776, Shawnee Indians kidnapped Boone's teenage daughter,
Jemima. They also took two other girls. "You
will be slaves," they said.

But Jemima Boone stared boldly at the red men. "My father will rescue us," she said.

The brave girls left a trail of torn bits of cloth. For two days, Daniel Boone and his men tracked the Indians and the captive girls. At last they caught up to them. Boone raised his rifle, Tick-Licker, took aim and fired.

One Indian fell dead. The others tried to kill the girls, but the settlers drove them away. The girls returned to Boonesborough unharmed.

Not long afterward, Boone received news from the east. On July 4, 1776, America had declared its independence from Britain.

It meant another war on the frontier. The British urged the Indians to fight the settlers. And the Indians were only too happy to wage war. Many tribes were angry about the new settlements of Kentucky. The white people cut down the forest and killed the animals. They would have to die!

Blackfish, chief of the Shawnee, planned to destroy all the white towns in Kentucky. He captured Boone and tried to force him to betray Boonesborough. But Boone escaped and helped the settlers beat off a ten-day Indian attack.

For the next four years there was terror in Kentucky. The land was called "the dark and bloody ground."

24

Despite the Indian raids, settlers kept on coming to Kentucky. Boone was now a famous man. He was elected to the assembly and owned thousands of acres of land.

In 1782, the Revolutionary War ended. Most of the hostile Indians retreated across

the Ohio River. Daniel and Rebecca Boone looked forward to a life of peace.

WESTWARD TO MISSOURI

But before long, disaster befell the pioneer hero. There was trouble over his land. He had never obtained legal title to it. Now lawyers told him that he did not own it after all.

Years of lawsuits followed. Little by little, all Boone's good land was taken away. He was a bitter old man. ''I could lick the Injuns,'' he said, ''but not these city lawyers!''

He began to think about following a new kind of Wilderness Road—one that led westward beyond the Mississippi. The land there belonged to Spain. Would an old frontiersman be welcome?

He sent his son, Daniel Morgan Boone, to the Spanish governor. The young man came back with a letter that said Boone would be most welcome. The Spanish would give him a large grant of land.

28

In 1799, he and Rebecca set out for
Missouri. Somebody asked why he was leaving

Kentucky. He said: "Too crowded! I want more elbow room!"

He established a new town on the Missouri.

For several years he lived there happily. His married children and many other settlers joined him. But then Spain turned the Missouri lands over to France—and France sold them to the United States. Poor Daniel Boone lost his land again.

He could still hunt and trap, so this is what he did for a living, until he was 80. He died in 1820, one of the greatest of American pioneers.

GALLERY OF GREAT AMERICANS SERIES